NOT A SILENT NIGHT
LEADER GUIDE

Not a Silent Night
Mary Looks Back to Bethlehem

Book
Not a Silent Night
978-1-426-77184-2   Also available as an eBook
Not a Silent Night: Large Print Edition
978-1-630-88295-2

DVD
Not a Silent Night: DVD
978-1-426-77185-9

Leader Guide
Not a Silent Night: Leader Guide
978-1-426-77199-6   Also available as an eBook

For more information, visit www.AdamHamilton.org.

Also by Adam Hamilton

24 Hours That Changed the World

Christianity and World Religions

Christianity's Family Tree

Confronting the Controversies

Enough

Final Words from the Cross

Forgiveness

Leading Beyond the Walls

Love to Stay

Making Sense of the Bible

Revival

Seeing Gray in a World of Black and White

Selling Swimsuits in the Arctic

The Journey

The Way

Unleashing the Word

When Christians Get It Wrong

Why?

ADAM HAMILTON

NOT A
SILENT NIGHT

MARY LOOKS BACK TO BETHLEHEM

LEADER GUIDE

BY MARTHA BETTIS GEE

Abingdon Press / Nashville

NOT A SILENT NIGHT:
MARY LOOKS BACK TO BETHLEHEM
LEADER GUIDE

Copyright © 2014 Abingdon Press
All rights reserved.

This book is printed on elemental, chlorine-free paper.

ISBN 978-1-426-77199-6

All Scripture quotations, unless otherwise indicated, are taken from the New Revised Standard Version of the Bible, copyright 1989, Division of Christian Education of the National Council of the Churches of Christ in the United States of America. Used by permission. All rights reserved.

14 15 16 17 18 19 20 21 22 23 — 10 9 8 7 6 5 4 3 2

MANUFACTURED IN THE UNITED STATES OF AMERICA

CONTENTS

TO THE LEADER

Welcome! In this study, you have the opportunity to facilitate a group of learners as they explore the meaning of Christmas through the lens of Mary, the mother of Jesus, in Adam Hamilton's book and video study *Not a Silent Night: Mary Looks Back to Bethlehem*.

As Hamilton tells us, no one was closer to Jesus than Mary, and no one shaped his life more than she. Because no one knew him better or loved him more, no one paid a bigger price for his birth, life, and death than his mother. Though we may have formed the impression that Mary's life was blessed, peaceful, and blissful, it was also challenging and painful. At times, it was filled with sorrow. Yet even in the face of pain and adversity, Mary would magnify the Lord and rejoice in God her Savior.

Beginning with what Scripture and early church tradition tell us about the end of Mary's life, then moving backward, the five sessions of this study will recount Mary's story, ending on Christmas with the birth of Jesus. In the process, learners will gain a new perspective of the beloved Christmas story and its connection to Christ's life, death, and resurrection.

This five-session study makes use of the following components:

- Adam Hamilton's book *Not a Silent Night;*

- a DVD containing videos in which Hamilton, using stories and Scripture, presents and expands upon some key points from the book;

- this Leader Guide.

Participants in the study also will need Bibles. If possible, notify those interested in the study in advance of the first session. Make arrangements for participants to get copies of the book so that they can read Chapter 1.

Using This Guide with Your Group

Scripture tells us that where two or three are gathered together, we can be assured of the presence of the Holy Spirit working in and through all those gathered. As you prepare to lead, pray for that presence and expect that you will experience it.

Because no two groups are alike, this guide has been designed to give you as study leader some flexibility and choice in tailoring the sessions for your group. The session format is listed below. You may choose any or all of the activities, adapting them as you wish to meet the schedule and needs of your particular group.

In the book and videos, participants will discover a rich offering of information presented in an accessible way. As study leader, you will want to tailor your session activities to the needs and interests of your particular group, as well as to the time frame you have available.

Session Format

Planning the Session

> Session Goals
> Biblical Foundation
> Special Preparation

Getting Started

> Opening Activity
> Opening Prayer

Learning Together

> Video Study and Discussion
> Bible and Book Study and Discussion

Wrapping Up

> Closing Activity
> Closing Prayer

Helpful Hints

Preparing for the Session

- Pray for the leading of the Holy Spirit as you prepare for the study. Pray for discernment for yourself and for each member of the study group.

- Before each session, familiarize yourself with the content. Read the week's book chapters again and watch the video segment.

- Choose the session elements you will use during the group session, including the specific discussion questions you plan to cover. Be prepared, however, to adjust the session as group members interact and as questions arise. Prepare carefully, but allow space for the Holy Spirit to move through the group members and through you as facilitator.

- Secure a TV and DVD player in advance.

- Prepare the space where the session will be held so that it will enhance the learning process. Ideally, group members should be seated around a table or in a circle so that all can see each other. Movable chairs are best, because the group may form pairs or small groups for discussion.

- Bring a supply of Bibles for those who forget to bring their own. Having a variety of Bible translations is helpful.

- For most sessions you will also need a chalkboard and chalk, a whiteboard and markers, or an easel with paper and markers.

Shaping the Learning Environment

- Create a climate of openness, encouraging group members to participate as they feel comfortable. Remember that some persons will jump right in with answers and comments, while others need time to process what is being discussed.

- If you notice that some group members never seem able to enter the conversation, ask them if they have thoughts to share. Give everyone a chance to talk, but keep the conversation moving. Moderate to prevent a few individuals from doing all the talking.

- Communicate the importance of group discussions and group exercises.

- If no one answers at first during discussions, do not be afraid of a silence. Count silently to ten; then say something such as, "Would anyone like to go first?" If no one responds, venture an answer yourself and ask for comments.

- Model openness as you share with the group. Group members will follow your example. If you limit your sharing to a surface level, you'll discover that others will do the same.

- Encourage multiple answers or responses before moving on.

- To help continue a discussion and give it greater depth, ask, "Why?" or "Why do you believe that?" or "Can you say more about that?"

- Affirm others' responses with comments such as "Great" or "Thanks" or "Good insight"—especially if this is the first time someone has spoken during the group session.

- Monitor your own contributions. If you are doing most of the talking, back off so that you do not train the group to listen rather than speak up.

- Remember that you don't have all the answers. Your job is to encourage discussion and participation.

Managing the Session

- Begin and end on time. If a session is running longer than expected, get consensus from the group before continuing beyond the agreed-upon ending time.

- Involve group members in various aspects of the group session, such as playing the DVD, saying prayers, or reading Scripture.

- Note that some sessions may call for breaking into smaller groups or pairs. This gives everyone a chance to speak and participate fully. Mix up the groups; don't let the same people pair up for every activity.

- The study will be most successful if group members treat one another with respect and are willing to listen to opinions that differ from their own. Work to ensure that the study offers a safe space for exploring the Bible.

SPECIAL PREPARATION

The Advent Wreath

Create an Advent wreath for classroom use over the course of the study, using the directions below. For those who want to use an Advent wreath at home, print the reproducible handout on the opposite page.

Get an evergreen wreath and space four purple candles evenly around its circumference. You will also need a white pillar candle, the Christ candle. A grapevine wreath can be used in place of the evergreen wreath, since the bare vines can also be a symbol of the potential of everlasting life. Depending on your church's regulations concerning lighted candles, battery-operated candles are a good substitute for open flames.

Many study groups will begin this study the week prior to the beginning of Advent on Christ the King Sunday. In that case, you may want to set up the wreath, but light only the Christ candle in the opening activity of the first session. If you begin the study at a different time, adjust the number of candles you light to fit the appropriate week of Advent.

Regardless of the wreath used, it can serve as a reminder of how we wait during the season of Advent for Christ's birth. Light one additional candle each week of Advent until all four shine brightly as a sign of the coming of Jesus Christ, the light of the world.

USING AN ADVENT WREATH AT HOME

Place four candles in a circle on an evergreen wreath or grapevine wreath. Traditionally the candles are purple, the color of royalty, signifying the coming of the King. Blue candles can be substituted. In the center, place a white candle, the Christ candle.

Families of any size and configuration can make use of the wreath as a way of centering their prayer or devotion time during Advent. While some Christians light the candles only on Sunday, others have found that lighting the candles daily can be a reminder of the quiet, reflective waiting and preparation valued by Christians in the midst of the consumerist frenzy of the culture. Here are a few suggestions for using the Advent wreath:

- In families with young children, use the wreath at mealtimes. Just light the candle (or candles) and say a simple blessing such as "Come, Lord Jesus, be our guest and let this meal to us be blest." Lighting the candle at bedtime can also be a way of winding down and focusing for all family members after a hectic day.

- With older children, make this a time to read a short Bible passage and have a prayer. Your congregation may have brief Advent wreath rituals or devotions for use by families. But in many families these days, schedules make even a brief time of devotion difficult. Try making a table tent with a Bible verse, and place it where busy family members grab a meal.

- Couples and single adults can use the wreath as a focal point for their time of devotions. In a busy and hectic schedule, an adult can simply light the candles and have a time of silent reflection before a meal. However you choose to use the wreath, make it a time to slow down, reflect, and savor the silence.

1.

Beginning with the End

Planning the Session

Session Goals

As a result of conversations and activities connected with this session, group members should:

- be introduced to an exploration of Christmas through the lens of Mary, Jesus' mother;

- reflect on Advent as the church's response to the amnesia that is the loss of the meaning of Christmas;

- explore traditions concerning the end of Mary's life and imagine the mission in which she might have been engaged;

- encounter the hope of Christmas embodied in the resurrection from the dead;

- be introduced to and commit to one or more Advent practices that embody hope.

Biblical Foundation

"You will receive power when the Holy Spirit has come upon you; and you will be my witnesses in Jerusalem, in all Judea and Samaria, and to the ends of the earth." When he [Jesus] had said this, as they were watching, he was lifted up, and a cloud took him out of their sight. While he was going and they were gazing up toward heaven, suddenly two men in white robes stood by them. They said, "Men of Galilee, why do you stand looking up toward heaven? This Jesus, who has been taken up from you into heaven, will come in the same way as you saw him go into heaven." *Revelation / white chariot*

Then they returned to Jerusalem from the mount called Olivet, which is near Jerusalem, a sabbath day's journey away. When they had entered the city, they went to the room upstairs where they were staying, Peter, and John, and James, and Andrew, Philip and Thomas, Bartholomew and Matthew, James son of Alphaeus, and Simon the Zealot, and Judas son of James. All these were constantly devoting themselves to prayer, together with certain women, including Mary the mother of Jesus, as well as his brothers. (Acts 1:8-14)

Special Preparation

- Set up an Advent wreath centered with a white pillar candle (see "To the Leader" under the Special Preparation header for more instructions).

- Make copies of the reproducible handout, "Using an Advent Wreath at Home" to distribute at the first class session.

- Collect ads for Christmas season shopping from the newspaper, or download from the Internet.

- If possible, locate and download some images of Mary from the Internet. Either make prints to show or get equipment to project them for the group.

- On a large sheet of paper, print the headings "Dormition" and "Assumption."

- This chapter includes the reflections of a mother who lost her son in a tragic accident. If your group includes parents who have lost a child of any age, be sensitive to how they may experience the discussion. Allow for a space that invites their own reflections if they so choose without putting them on the spot.

- Remember that there are more activities than most groups will have time to complete. As leader, you'll want to go over the session in advance and select or adapt the activities you think will work best for your group in the time allotted.

Getting Started

Opening Activity

As participants arrive, welcome them to the study. If group members are not familiar with one another, make nametags available. Provide Bibles for those who did not bring one.

Invite group members to introduce themselves. Ask each to respond to this open-ended prompt: "It's only a few weeks until Christmas, and I'm feeling . . ."

When everyone has had the chance to respond, talk together about what everyone's responses reveal. Who is feeling positive? Who is anticipating a special Christmas? Who is feeling the stress of not enough time to get ready, of tasks unfinished? How many are uneasy about the money they are spending on gifts? Who is feeling rushed, depressed, even a little angry?

Write the term "Black Friday" on a board or paper. To what does the phrase refer? Invite participants to share their experiences—positive or negative—either on Black Friday or since that time.

Distribute the copies of ads. Ask:

- What do the ads communicate about the coming holiday?

- Imagine you have been transported from another planet to this community. How would you describe the approaching holiday? What might you say is its purpose? What "good news of great joy" do you see?

Ask a volunteer to summarize the account of what happened to Jdimytai Damour. Adam Hamilton tells us that this story is the symbol of something bigger—a kind of amnesia. What does he mean?

Invite the group to silently read the paragraph in which Hamilton describes Advent. On a large sheet of paper or on the board, print the following phrase: "Advent is . . ." and ask participants to call out words or phrases that come to mind about the season of Advent. Jot these down.

Depending on when you are beginning this study (prior to the beginning of Advent or the first week of Advent), light either the first candle on the Advent wreath or the Christ candle that is in the center of the wreath.

[handwritten notes: Advent / A Time of Hope / I Time to remember old friends]

Opening Prayer

Say, "Come, Lord Jesus." Allow for a time of silence. Then pray:

Come, Lord Jesus. We look forward to the time when you will come again at Christmas. We wait in hope for that day when you will come again in glory. By your Spirit, help us to prepare in ways that honor that hope. It is in your name we pray. Amen.

Learning Together

Video Study and Discussion

Briefly introduce Adam Hamilton, the author of the study. Hamilton is senior pastor of The United Methodist Church of the Resurrection in Leawood, Kansas, where he preaches to more than eight thousand people per week. Hamilton is known for helping those striving to be Christians see the implications of the gospel for daily life. If participants have smartphones, they can learn more about Hamilton and other books he has authored at www.adamhamilton.org.

In this study, Hamilton invites us to look at Christmas and its meaning through the lens of the life of Mary. But, as he points out, the study will start not by looking at the beginning of the story, but at its end. Each successive week, the group will travel back in Mary's life—from the Crucifixion and Resurrection, to Jesus' life and ministry, to his discovery at the Temple when he was twelve, to the appearance of the angel Gabriel, until finally, on Christmas Day, they will read about and consider the birth of the Christ Child.

Session 1 begins at the end of Mary's life, imagining, based on Scripture and tradition, what Mary did in the years after Jesus' crucifixion and resurrection.

Before the video, introduce the subject of Advent, asking participants whether as children they celebrated Advent or knew what Advent was. Discuss the meaning of Advent as they understand it now.

After viewing the video, ask participants to share their responses to the story of the Walmart employee, Jdimytai Damour. Discuss:

- What examples have you seen of people mistreating each other while Christmas shopping? *Hurting*
- What do these incidents tell us about our culture, and what can we do about it?

This study takes an unusual look at Christmas: through the lens of Mary. Discuss:

- What can we observe from Mary's perspective that we may not have thought about before?
- How do you feel about the use of church tradition (Roman Catholic and Eastern Orthodox) to fill in parts of her life that aren't covered by Scripture? What are advantages and disadvantages of doing so?

never had other children

Bible and Book Study and Discussion

Explore Early Church Traditions about Mary

Hamilton notes that we know very little about the end of Mary's life and so are left with traditions that evolved in the early church. Form two groups. Ask one group to read the material in the text under the heading "Mary's Final Years," describing Catholic traditions; and ask the other group to read about Orthodox traditions.

After allowing a few minutes for groups to read, ask each one to report what the traditions tell us. Write what they say on the large sheet of paper you prepared in advance. Invite participants to tell what they think about the various views of Mary's death and to offer opinions on what her burial location communicates about Mary. Then discuss:

- Hamilton observes that Protestants tend to be more cautious about traditions such as these. What does he say about the focus of such stories? What do you think?

- The author also notes that Christmas and Easter are a package deal. What does he mean?

Read Gospel Accounts of the Resurrection

Form small groups of four participants and assign one of the following passages to each of the four participants in all the groups: Matthew 27:55; 28:1-10; Mark 15:40; 16:1-8; Luke 23:55; 24:1-12; John 19:25-26, 20:1-10. Ask participants to scan their assigned Gospel account to see which women were reported to have been witnesses at the Crucifixion and at the empty tomb. Discuss:

- Based on the four Gospel accounts, we cannot be sure that Mary was present on the first Easter morning. The same can be said about her presence at the Crucifixion. What do you think?

- What do you think of Pope John Paul II's suggestion about Jesus appearing to his mother before appearing to anyone else?

Discuss Experiences of Grief and Resurrection Hope

In "The Hope of Resurrection," invite the group to read silently the quotation from the woman who experienced the death of a son, as well as the paragraph where Hamilton describes the experience of being present at his grandfather's death. Discuss:

- Hamilton suggests that the hope Mary experienced in the Resurrection transformed the grief, separation, and loss she carried with her following Jesus' death. How do you respond?

Invite group members who are willing to do so to talk about their own losses of loved ones and how the hope of resurrection has played a part in how they experienced grief.

Ask the group to read silently the references that are included in the text from 1 Thessalonians 4:13-14, 16-18 and 1 Corinthians 15:54. Discuss:

- What are the encouragements the author notes in these passages, and how are they part of the promise and hope of Christmas?

Encounter the Early Church's Mission

This week's Bible text includes the Matthew verses we call the Great Commission and notes that Luke, the writer of the Book of Acts, tells the story a little differently. Ask the group to read silently Acts 1:1-7. Invite a volunteer to read aloud this session's biblical foundation, Acts 1:8-14. Discuss:

- What were Jesus' followers doing to prepare for the promised coming of the Holy Spirit? What did they do afterward to launch the church?

- Hamilton poses the question: What do you think Mary was up to from the time that Jesus ascended to heaven until her own death? How would you imagine she responded to her son's call to be a part of God's mission?

- What are we doing, as individuals and as a church, to prepare for the coming of Jesus Christ at Christmas?

- Hamilton suggests that if our Christmas does not include serving the poor in some way, we are missing out on part of our mission. How are we working or could we work to bring hope to the world by focusing on the commission we have been given?

Wrapping Up

Hamilton invites us to return to the tragic account of Jdimytai Damour's death in the Walmart stampede, noting that of the two thousand people in the crowd, only a handful stopped to try to create a barricade around his body. Invite the group to reflect on his questions:

- Why do you think so few people stopped?

- Would you have stopped?

Encourage the group members to think about ways they might offer hope, encouragement, and joy to others at this season and how they might embody the mission of Christmas. Ask them to suggest specific ways to do so in the coming week, and list these on a large sheet of paper. You might suggest the following as well:

1. Make a family Advent wreath and light one candle in the coming week, praying for hope and consolation. Distribute the reproducible handout "Using an Advent Wreath at Home."

2. Consider inviting a person who is alone this season to come for a family meal.

3. Although it is late in the shopping season to do so, sit down as a family and consider whether

consumption is consuming your time, energy, and resources. How might you take one small step to observe the season more simply?

7. Invite an older relative or church member for coffee and cookies, and ask that person to share reminiscences of childhood Christmases. What is the same in today's Christmas? What is different?

Closing Activity

If you have downloaded images of Mary to print or project, display them now, inviting the group to reflect on what the images communicate about Mary. Light the candle again and allow for a time of silence. Invite participants to respond to the following: "In Advent, my hope for myself is . . . my hope for others is . . . my hope for the world is . . . "

Encourage participants to read Chapter 2 before the next session.

Closing Prayer

Come, Lord Jesus. By your Spirit, guide us to spaces where we can experience silence. Give us resurrection hope—the assurance that we will see you and that we will see those we love again. Give us the hope that things will not always be as they are now. Stir us up to embrace your mission for the world, that in your good time everything will be set right. In your name we pray. Amen.

2.

THE PIERCING
OF MARY'S SOUL

Planning the Session

Session Goals

As a result of conversations and activities connected with this session, group members should:

- continue an exploration of Christmas through the lens of Mary, Jesus' mother;

- experience and imagine, through walking the Stations of the Cross, what might have been in Mary's heart and mind as she witnessed Jesus' arrest, trial, crucifixion, and death;

- note the significance of things that were said about Jesus before his birth and immediately after, and connect those with accounts of his crucifixion and death;

- explore the meaning of the cross and sacrifice;

- expand their understanding of sin;

- give thanks for the costly gift of Jesus' life, given freely for our sins;

- be introduced to and commit to further ways to prepare for Christmas in Advent.

Biblical Foundation

The child's father and mother were amazed at what was being said about him. Then Simeon blessed them and said to his mother Mary, "This child is destined for the falling and the rising of many in Israel, and to be a sign that will be opposed so that the inner thoughts of many will be revealed—and a sword will pierce your own soul too." (Luke 2:33-35)

Special Preparation

- If possible, locate and download an image of Michelangelo's *Pietà* from the Internet. Make a print of the image, mount it on construction paper or posterboard, and display it for the Stations of the Cross activity.

- To set up the Stations of the Cross, make the following signs: The Home of the High Priest, The Palace of Pontius Pilate, The Palace Guard, and Golgotha.

Post the signs in that order at intervals around your
learning space. At each station, place a battery-
operated candle (optional). If you like, recruit
participants in advance to read aloud the book text
associated with each station: Station 1: paragraphs
1 and 2 under the heading "The Day Mary's Soul Was
Pierced"; Station 2: paragraph 3; Station 3: paragraphs
4 and 5; Station 4: paragraphs 6,7,8.

• Remember that there are more activities than most
groups will have time to complete. As leader, you'll
want to go over the session in advance and select or
adapt the activities you think will work best for your
group in the time allotted.

Getting Started

Opening Activity

Welcome participants and introduce any newcomers. Provide Bibles for those who did not bring one.

Gather together. Remind participants that for this
Advent study, the author invites us to view Christmas
through the lens of Mary, the mother of Jesus. In the
first session, the group began at the end, encountering in traditions of the church and in a passage from
Acts what the end of Mary's life might have been like.
In today's session, through scriptural accounts, they
will examine the narratives of the Crucifixion and
imagine that event through Mary's eyes.

Invite participants to imagine they are the parents of a son who has been convicted of a capital crime, but who is innocent. Ask volunteers to describe how they believe such a mother or father would feel as a witness to these events:

- being present to see their son on trial for his life;

- hearing him convicted, then sentenced;

- observing his execution.

It is probable that Mary experienced very similar emotions to those the group imagined. In this session the group will be introduced to the events of Jesus' trial and death from a different perspective than they have perhaps ever experienced—the intimate personal perspective of a mother.

Opening Prayer

Light one candle (or the appropriate number of candles for this week) on the Advent wreath with the words, "Come, Lord Jesus." Allow for a time of silence. Then pray:

Come, Lord Jesus. We give thanks for the gift of your life, freely given for us. Guide us to prepare for the celebration of your birth in ways that honor that gift. In your name we pray. Amen.

Learning Together

Video Study and Discussion

Session 2 imagines what Mary was thinking and feeling as she watched the Crucifixion from the foot of the cross and suggests some things we can learn about Christmas by doing so.

Before viewing the video, tell participants that in this session, we take the unusual approach of discussing the Crucifixion in a program about Advent and Christmas. Ask the class to speculate on why we're doing this and what might be learned.

After the video, ask participants again to consider the effect of looking through Mary's eyes. Discuss:

- What unique insights can we gain by viewing the crucifixion of Jesus and the hours leading up to it from Mary's perspective, as opposed to, say, Peter's or another disciple's?

- Hamilton speculates that while watching the crucifixion of Jesus, Mary may have been thinking of Christmas. What do you think of that observation? What other thoughts and feelings may have been going through Mary's mind?

- Think about Michelangelo's *Pietà*. How do you respond to the image of Jesus on his grieving mother's lap? What do you appreciate about this pietà?

Bible and Book Study and Discussion

Ask a volunteer to read aloud the biblical foundation for the session, Luke 2:33-35. Call attention to the session title and to the last phrase in the passage that refers to the piercing of Mary's soul. Invite the group to consider the events of Jesus' crucifixion and how those events must surely have pierced Mary's soul, just as Simeon prophesied.

Walk the Stations of the Cross

Remind the group that in the previous session, Adam Hamilton contended that Christmas and Easter are a package deal.

In Holy Week (most often on Good Friday), Christians will undertake to walk the Stations of the Cross. Sometimes called the Way of the Cross, the Via Dolorosa, or the Way of Sorrows, the activity traditionally refers to a series of artistic representations showing Christ carrying his cross to site of the Crucifixion. The tradition of moving around the stations to reenact the Passion of Christ began with St. Francis of Assisi. Today the practice is observed in a variety of ways, but most often it involves praying at each station.

In order to experience what the text has to say about Mary at the cross, participants will experience a modified version of the stations. Point out the posted signs and candles. Describe how the walk will take place: the entire group will move together to each station in order, stopping so the recruited readers can offer the text for reflection. The group will pause in silence for prayer at each station before moving on to the next.

Explore Thoughts of Christmas

Hamilton imagines what Mary might have been thinking during the six hours when Jesus was hanging on the cross. Invite participants to respond to the following ponderings and thoughts that Mary might have had:

- What is the meaning and significance of Jesus' name?

- What was communicated by the shepherds about who Jesus would become?

- In what ways did Jesus' birth bring good tidings of great joy, and for whom?

- What did it mean that Jesus was destined for the rising and falling of many in Israel?

- Why was myrrh a strange gift for a child but a significant one for Jesus?

- Why does Hamilton believe Mary might have been remembering these events during the six hours she kept vigil at the foot of the cross? What is your response to his suggestion?

- Do you think Mary understood all that happened as she watched her son die? Why or why not?

- At the end of Luke's account of Jesus' birth, he reports that "Mary treasured all these words and pondered them in her heart." Do you agree with Hamilton that she probably looked back on those events and pondered their meaning in the light of Jesus' crucifixion? Why or why not?

- Hamilton notes that the disciples likely did not understand the events they had experienced until after Jesus' resurrection. Read Isaiah 53:3-5. To whom or what was it probably referring when its original audience heard it? How might the disciples have interpreted that passage following Jesus' resurrection?

Examine Sacrifice Imagery

Hamilton confesses that the ways Jesus' death might bring about our forgiveness is something of an enigma. Invite a volunteer or two to summarize what the book has to say in explaining the significance of blood sacrifices to first-century people. Discuss:

- Hamilton speaks of the cross as a pronouncement about human sin and an indictment on us. What does he mean?

- What is the message of the cross for those who feel guilty? What is its message, if any, for those who do not feel guilty and do not understand the idea of the cross?

- How is sin defined here? In what ways are we complicit in what happens in the world around us— in the broken, alienated places and in the wide disparities that divide people?

- Recall the discussions in Session 1 about the consumption that seems to consume us during this time of year. In what ways are we complicit in further dividing the haves and have-nots through our conspicuous consumption? What connections can you make between what happens on Black Friday and what happened on Good Friday?

- Hamilton observes that the cross only makes sense when you begin to have a realistic picture of human sin. How do you respond? How do you describe human sin?

Ask someone to read aloud Romans 5:1, 6, 8. Invite the group to reflect in silence on the seriousness of our sin, the costliness of our forgiveness, and the magnitude of God's love.

Wrapping Up

Invite participants to respond and complete this open-ended sentence: "As I think back over this session, I believe I will continue to ponder . . ."

Ask participants to consider how they might respond to the magnitude of God's love as they continue to prepare for the coming of Christ at Christmas. In addition, give them the following suggestions:

1. As they light candles this week on the Advent wreath, invite them to read aloud the next-to-last paragraph in this chapter ("Our Advent journey, preparing our hearts to celebrate the gift of Jesus Christ . . ."). Offer a prayer of gratitude to God for the gift of salvation in Jesus Christ.

2. Hamilton notes that just as Christmas and Easter are a package, so it is impossible to separate Christmas and the cross. He describes an ornament on his family Christmas tree—a simple spike as a reminder of how Jesus was nailed to the cross. Create a simple ornament with two large nails, overlapped and fastened together with wire to form a cross, and hang it on your Christmas tree as a reminder of the connection between the cradle and the cross.

3. Talk together as a family about the expectations everyone has for gifts. In what ways might you step back from conspicuous consumption? To what mission projects or church endeavors might you give a monetary gift, perhaps dedicating a portion of what you had planned to spend? What gifts might you buy from Fair Trade organizations that could benefit artisans seeking to improve their own lives?

Closing Activity

Again light the Advent candles and allow for a time of silence. Encourage participants to read Chapter 3 before the next session.

Closing Prayer

Come, Lord Jesus. We give thanks for the costly gift of your life, given freely for our sins. By your Spirit, guide us as we seek ways to prepare for your coming at Christmas. As we try to live out our calling in the midst of the glitter and confusion of the Christmas season, help us to keep the cross at the center of our vision. In your name we pray. Amen.

3.

Amazed, Astounded, and Astonished

Planning the Session

Session Goals

As a result of conversations and activities connected with this session, group members should:

- continue an exploration of Christmas through the lens of Mary, Jesus' mother;

- imagine the emotions Mary must have been feeling when Jesus could not be found in Jerusalem and when she and Joseph finally discovered him in the Temple;

- be introduced to the significance this event had as a defining moment in which Jesus came to accept and embrace his calling;

- encounter more fully the impact of Jesus' words and deeds through a study of two Greek words;

- begin to explore what it means to follow Jesus;

- be introduced to and commit to more ways of preparing for Christmas in Advent.

Biblical Foundation

Now every year his [Jesus'] parents went to Jerusalem for the festival of the Passover. And when he was twelve years old, they went up as usual for the festival. When the festival was ended and they started to return, the boy Jesus stayed behind in Jerusalem, but his parents did not know it. Assuming that he was in the group of travelers, they went a day's journey. Then they started to look for him among their relatives and friends. When they did not find him, they returned to Jerusalem to search for him. After three days they found him in the temple, sitting among the teachers, listening to them and asking them questions. And all who heard him were amazed at his understanding and his answers. When his parents saw him they were astonished; and his mother said to him, "Child, why have you treated us like this? Look, your father and I have been searching for you in great anxiety." He said to them, "Why were you searching for me? Did you not know that I must be in my Father's house?" But they did not understand what he said to them. Then he went down with them and came to Nazareth, and was obedient to them. His mother treasured all these things in her heart. (Luke 2:41-51)

Special Preparation

- It would be helpful (though not essential) to have available a map of first-century Palestine.

- A suggested wrap-up activity is to sing the old hymn "Wonderful Words of Life." Locate the hymn in a hymnal or download it from the Internet.

- A portion of the discussion in this chapter focuses on the difficulty of parenting. Be aware of those in your group who may be single or who may be childless, whether by choice or not. For those participants, shift the focus to their memories of the parenting challenges they may have posed for their own parents.

- Remember that there are more activities than most groups will have time to complete. As leader, you'll want to go over the session in advance and select—or adapt—the activities you think will work best for your group in the time allotted.

Getting Started

Opening Activity

Welcome participants and introduce any newcomers. Provide Bibles for those who did not bring one. Gather together. Remind participants that for this Advent study, the author invites us to view Christmas through the lens of Mary, the mother of Jesus.

In Session 1, the group began at the end, encountering in traditions of the church and in a passage from Acts what the end of Mary's life might have been like. In Session 2, they imagined the narratives of the Crucifixion through the eyes of Mary. In today's session, the group will explore the one story that is included in Scripture about Jesus as a boy.

Invite participants to bring to mind a time when they were terribly worried about a child who was late coming home, or who was lost. For group members who are not parents, ask them to recall a time from childhood or adolescence when something like that happened to them. Form pairs and ask participants to tell their partner what happened. Back in the large group, ask a volunteer or two to tell how they felt— or how they imagine their parents felt—and how the situation was resolved.

Invite the group to scan through Hamilton's account of the time his six-year-old daughter was left behind. How do the feelings recalled and shared in your group compare with what Hamilton experienced?

Tell the group that today's biblical foundation is a similar story about Jesus.

Opening Prayer

Light the appropriate number of candles on the Advent wreath with the words, "Come, Lord Jesus." Allow for a time of silence. Then pray:

Come, Lord Jesus. Be with us today as we prepare for the celebration of your birth. Open our eyes to the way in which you would have us live, not only in the weeks before celebrating Christmas but in our day-to-day lives as Christians. In your name we pray. Amen.

Learning Together

Video Study and Discussion

In Session 3, we go back to Jesus' boyhood and the one childhood story about him that is given in the Bible: Jesus' staying behind in Jerusalem and being discovered by his frantic parents while he was sitting among the teachers.

Before viewing the video, ask participants to recall and share some of the earliest memories of their own or, if they have children, of their kids, noting that sometimes the things we remember most vividly are painful experiences.

After viewing the video, discuss Mary and Joseph's traumatic experience in parenting. Discuss:

- How would you have felt in their situation? What might you have done differently?

- What would your reaction have been when you finally found your son?

This study is marked by unusual perspectives. In the story of Jesus in the Temple, imagine the events from the perspective of those who heard twelve-year-old Jesus ask and answer questions of the teachers. Discuss:

- What would you have thought and how would you have felt listening to Jesus? Can you think of a modern-day equivalent of this situation?

- What do you imagine they heard Jesus saying? How might it have been different from the other teachers in the Temple?

Bible and Book Study and Discussion

Explore Scripture

To set the stage for hearing the Scripture read, give the group some context. If you have a map of Palestine, have someone point out the town of Nazareth and the city of Jerusalem. The distance between them is ninety-five miles, a journey of three or four days by caravan. The text tells us that it was required for every male Jew within a reasonable distance to make the pilgrimage to Jerusalem for Passover, perhaps similar to the practice of modern-day Muslims who make a pilgrimage to Mecca for Hajj.

As a volunteer reads Luke 2:41-44 aloud, invite the group to imagine they are part of the caravan on the road home from Jerusalem. After the reading, ask participants to respond to the following:

- As you imagined the story, where and who were you?

- As you traveled, what did you see? hear? smell?

- How did you feel when Mary and Joseph went look-ing for their son, Jesus? How did they act?

Now ask a volunteer to continue reading verses 45-51 and ask the group to imagine they are Jesus' parents. Discuss the following:

- Hamilton observes that Mary and Joseph searched frantically for three days. He suggests that the Gospel writer mentions the time frame because it points to another period of grieving for Mary. How do you respond?

- Imagine that after a day of searching, Mary and Joseph put out an Amber Alert on Jesus. How do you think they would have described him? If asked to describe their son after they had found him in the Temple and heard him speaking, how might their description have changed? What fresh fears and concerns might Mary have had about parenting a son such as Jesus?

- Parenting can be hard. As in life, there are calm periods alternating with times of grief and pain. However, difficult and painful experiences in our own lives and those of our children are often defining moments that bring something good. Would you agree? Why or why not? Think of some examples from your own life.

Explore Word Meanings

On a large sheet of paper, print the Greek words *odunao* and *existemi*. Call the group's attention to this chapter's title. Form pairs, and in each pair ask each person to take one word. Have the pairs scan the chapter to find information about the meanings of their assigned word and where else in the Gospels the word is used. Each person should then briefly report on the assigned word to his or her partner. Then, in the large group, invite volunteers to comment on relevant information about the word and jot this down on the board or large sheet of paper. Discuss:

- In what ways does having a deeper knowledge of these words add to our understanding of the story?

- People were frequently astonished, astounded, even dumbfounded by the words and actions of Jesus. What do you think was the impact on Jesus' followers? How did the religious authorities respond?

Encounter Jesus in the Story

Some scholars believe this story is preserved in the Gospels because it marked a defining moment in which Jesus came to accept and embrace his calling.

- Didn't Jesus understand all along that he was the Son of God? What do you think? How is your answer

shaped by the fact that Jesus was fully human as well
as fully divine?

- Jesus' response to his mother when she told him they
  had been searching for him was that he had been in
  his Father's house. Why do you think the practice of
  calling God "Father" may be challenging for some?
  What did Hamilton learn about God from his own
  experience as a father? How do you respond to his
  views and statements?

Explore Words of Life—and the Way

Hamilton observes that some Christians act as if
all Jesus ever did was to be born, be crucified, and
be raised from the dead. They sometimes downplay
his life and ministry, referred to by his followers as
the Way.

- Christians were followers of the Way because Jesus
  offered a different way than the rest of the world
  offered. In our contemporary context, how would you
  describe the values and ethics that our culture seems
  to affirm—in other words, what is the "way" our
  modern world follows? What and who are seen to be
  important? How do Christians stand over and against
  those cultural values?

- Christians sometimes take for granted the things Jesus
  taught about how to live. What values and beliefs can
  you name that are part of following Jesus?

Wrapping Up

Invite the group to listen once more as you read today's biblical foundation passage (Luke 2:41-51). As they listen, ask them to imagine hearing twelve-year-old Jesus speak at the Temple. What questions would they like to ask him? After the reading, ask participants to share those questions.

One major focus of Jesus' teachings was the nature of God's kingdom and an invitation to be a part of it right now. These are words to live by. Sing or recite together the hymn "Wonderful Words of Life."

Ask participants to consider how they might respond to the call of Jesus, our Lord, to follow him and do as he commanded as they continue to prepare for the coming of Christ at Christmas. Also give them the following suggestions:

1. As they light candles this week on the Advent wreath, invite them to read aloud the following sentence: This is what we celebrate at Christmas— not only the hope of resurrection and the gift of salvation, but the map that helps the lost find their way, the light that helps illuminate our darkness, the truth that is worth everything to have. Read aloud John 1:1, 4, 14. Offer a prayer of gratitude to God for the words and actions of Jesus that teach us how to live.

2. Suggest to participants who are parents or grand-parents that they discuss with their children and

grandchildren ways in which the family might follow Jesus during Advent. What is the family being
called to embrace? to give up? Invite all group
members to listen carefully to children and youth
for ideas that may astound or amaze them.

3. As Christmas approaches and the frenzy
   accelerates, encourage group members to set aside
   intentionally some time for quiet reflection. Suggest
   that they use the phrase *Come, Lord Jesus* as a
   breath prayer, silently repeating the word *Come*
   as they inhale and the words *Lord Jesus* as they
   exhale. Hamilton observes that when we talk about
   Jesus as Savior, we're talking about the cross and
   his death. When we talk about Jesus as Lord, we're
   talking about his call to us to follow him and do as
   he commanded. Making space for silence invites
   deeper understandings of our call.

Closing Activity

Again light the Advent candles and allow for a time
of silence. Encourage participants to read Chapter 4
before the next session.

Closing Prayer

*Come, Lord Jesus. By your Spirit, guide us to a fuller
understanding of what it means to live for you. As we prepare
for your arrival at Christmas, make us ever more aware of
your words, and open our hearts to be amazed and astounded
by them. In your name we pray. Amen.*

4.

MARY, FULL OF GRACE

Planning the Session

Session Goals

As a result of conversations and activities connected with this session, group members should:

- continue an exploration of Christmas through the lens of Mary, Jesus' mother;

- compare the qualities that the world values with the qualities Mary embodied;

- explore God's preference for the lowly and for reversals of the expected, and examine the destructive role of pride;

- encounter and expand an understanding of God's grace as exemplified in Mary;

- be introduced to and commit to one or more Advent practices.

Biblical Foundation

In the sixth month the angel Gabriel was sent by God to a town in Galilee called Nazareth, to a virgin engaged to a man whose name was Joseph, of the house of David. The virgin's name was Mary. And he came to her and said, "Greetings, favored one! The Lord is with you." But she was much perplexed by his words and pondered what sort of greeting this might be. The angel said to her, "Do not be afraid, Mary, for you have found favor with God. And now, you will conceive in your womb and bear a son, and you will name him Jesus. He will be great, and will be called the Son of the Most High, and the Lord God will give to him the throne of his ancestor David. He will reign over the house of Jacob forever, and of his kingdom there will be no end." (Luke 1:26-33)

Special Preparation

- Two musical selections are suggested in this session, one for the opening activity and one for the wrap-up: "Breath of Heaven" and "Canticle of the Turning." Look up, print out, or post the lyrics to these songs, or make arrangements for the group to view them on YouTube.

- You will need writing paper and pens for participants, as well as large sheets of drawing paper and colored pens or crayons.

- Remember that there are more activities than most groups will have time to complete. As leader, you'll want to go over the session in advance and select or adapt the activities you think will work best for your group in the time allotted.

Getting Started

Opening Activity

As participants arrive, welcome them and greet any newcomers. Provide Bibles for those who did not bring one. Remind participants that for this Advent study, the author invites us to view Christmas through the lens of Mary, the mother of Jesus. The author has chosen to move backward in time, beginning in Session 1 at the end, exploring what the end of Mary's life might have been like. In Session 2, the group looked at the Crucifixion through the eyes of Mary. In Session 3, they recalled the story of twelve-year-old Jesus, left behind in Jerusalem and discovered by his frantic parents in the Temple talking with the teachers there. This session explores the day when Mary first learned she was going to have a child.

Point out the words to Amy Grant's song "Breath of Heaven," and invite the group to read the lyrics silently. If you have chosen to show a YouTube clip, ask the group to imagine themselves to be Mary as they view the clip.

Opening Prayer

Light the appropriate number of candles on the Advent wreath with the words, "Come, Lord Jesus." Allow for a time of silence. Then pray:

Come, Lord Jesus. By your Spirit, help us to prepare for your arrival at Christmas. Guide us as we seek to encounter you in Scripture, and give us new insights into familiar stories. In your name we pray. Amen.

Learning Together

Video Study and Discussion

Session 4 tells the story of Mary as a teenager to whom the angel Gabriel appears, telling her she will give birth to the son of God, and what this would mean for Mary and for us.

Before viewing the video, ask participants to recite some of the words of the hymn "Amazing Grace." In the hymn, what is grace, and what does it mean to the speaker? How do participants imagine that Mary's life was full of grace, when we have seen the pain she suffered?

After viewing the video, ask participants to recall examples of grace in their own lives, making sure they understand that grace is specifically unearned and not deserved. Discuss:

- The speaker in "Amazing Grace" describes himself as a wretch. Do you have to be a wretch to receive grace? Are we all wretches? If we're not, does grace mean any less?

- Describe an incident from your own life in which you experienced grace. What effect did it have on you? Do you view it differently now after the fact? What did you learn and can you learn from the experience?

In the video, Hamilton discusses pride and its pitfalls. Discuss:

- What are some times in your own life when, in retrospect, you committed the sin of pride? How did you respond, and what would you do differently today?

- Is pride always a sin? Are there times when pride is good?

Bible and Book Study and Discussion

Write a Job Description

Distribute writing paper and pens. Invite the group to set aside for the moment what they already know about Mary and instead to think objectively about what kind of mother might have been ideal for the Messiah the Jewish people longed for and expected. What sort of background would have helped her equip a son to challenge the powerful forces by which the people of Palestine were oppressed? Invite them to jot down qualifications and characteristics, as in a job description, that one might expect to be ideal.

After allowing a few minutes for participants to work, ask a volunteer or two to read what they wrote. Then ask participants to scan the information in the first paragraph of the book chapter, as well as the fourth paragraph under the heading "Why Mary?" On the back of the sheet, ask them to write a description of Mary. Discuss:

- In discussing why God chose Mary, Hamilton quotes Mary's famous Magnificat, the song she sang in reaction to Elizabeth's recognition of her baby. What do you think Mary's song has to do with God's choosing her? What can we learn from the Magnificat?

- According to Hamilton, why did God choose Mary? What qualifications did God seem to consider as paramount?

- Who else in the Bible does Hamilton name as unlikely choices to do important work for God? Can you think of other examples from Scripture?

- Do you think Mary had a choice of whether to become Jesus' mother? Why or why not?

Examine the Effects of Pride

Pride is a dangerous sin that eats away at the soul. Invite the group to discuss the following:

- What are the implications of this fact for those of us who are successful, who have means? What does he suggest is important for those in that category? What are the implications for those of us who downplay the importance of money and means?

- How are privilege and pride related? Where have you experienced people exercising privilege simply because they can? Give some examples. What was the result for you?

- The text notes that you either humble yourself, or you invite God to do it for you. Do you agree or disagree? Do you think the experience of being humbled is necessarily God's doing, or can it be the natural result of privileged pride, or can it be caused by something else?

Create a Visual Interpretation of the Meaning of Grace

Invite a volunteer to read Luke 1:26-33 aloud. On a board or large sheet of paper, print the Greek word *kecharitomene*. Hamilton tells us that this is the word translated as "favored one" or "full of grace." Its root is the word *charis*. He asks us to consider what *grace* means in the New Testament.

Invite the group to read over what the author says about grace under the heading "Full of Grace." Distribute drawing paper and colored pens or crayons to the group. Invite them to print the word grace in the center of the paper in large letters. Then ask them to choose words or phrases from this portion of the chapter and arrange them on the paper so they communicate what each person thinks grace is—what it encompasses, what its results are, how it functions in our lives, and so on. Allow time for participants to work, then ask them to display their word drawings. Invite them to take time to explore the work of other group members. Then ask for responses. Discuss:

- Grace has power—the power to change hearts, heal broken relationships, and reconcile people and even nations. Describe some examples of grace used in the book. What other stories of grace can you recall from the Bible and from our time?

- The blessed, God-favored, grace-filled life is still difficult and challenging sometimes. What were the difficulties and challenges for Mary? About what things did she have every reason to be fearful?

- Somehow God can bring blessing out of the pain a person is experiencing. Where have you experienced such blessing? If there are unhealed wounds in your past, what do you think is standing in the way of grace? What actions on your part might allow grace to flow, even in the present?

Wrapping Up

Invite the group to read silently Luke 2:39-45. Then invite them to read aloud in unison Mary's Magnificat in Luke 1:46-55. Sing or recite together the song that you prepared in advance, "A Canticle of the Turning," along with the video clip, or simply use the lyric sheet.

Ask participants to consider how they might respond to God's abundant grace—freely given to us although we do not deserve it—as they continue to prepare for the coming of Christ at Christmas. Also give them the following suggestions:

1. As they light candles this week on the Advent wreath, invite them to read aloud John 1:14, 16–17, emphasizing the word *grace* as they read.

2. Christmas is about grace, and Jesus came to show grace to humankind. When you receive grace, you're meant to give it away. Challenge participants to reflect on whether there is someone, either in their present or in their past, who has wronged them or hurt them and does not deserve to receive kindness. Ask participants to consider sending that person a Christmas card or a personal note. The card or note may allow them to let go of resentment, even if the person who wronged them is not changed by their action.

3. Invite participants, as a spiritual practice, to offer hospitality to someone they encounter who is perhaps living in more humble circumstances than they. In particular, challenge them to offer a personal greeting to persons serving them as cashiers, waitstaff, or other similar roles. Encourage them to be intentional about how they interact with these people.

Closing Activity

Again light the Advent candles and allow for a time of silence. Encourage participants to read Chapter 5 before the next session.

Closing Prayer

Come, Lord Jesus. By your Spirit, guide us to more grace-filled living, even as we acknowledge that we are undeserving of this rich gift. As we prepare for your coming at Christmas, give us humble spirits and loving hearts. In your name we pray. Amen.

5.

IT WAS NOT A SILENT NIGHT

Planning the Session

Session Goals

As a result of conversations and activities connected with this session, group members should:

- complete an exploration of Christmas through the lens of Mary, Jesus' mother;

- encounter the disparities between the idealized Christmas we yearn for and the realities of our messy, difficult, challenging lives at Christmas; between the perfect world we hope for and the broken world in which we live;

- compare and contrast contemporary birthing experiences and those of the first century, and explore implications for Mary;

- explore the real gifts of Christmas—the gift of the Way, the gift of love, the gift of forgiveness and new life, the gift of the Resurrection—and affirm that these offer us the truth about life;

- be introduced to and commit to practices that extend and deepen our lives as people of faith.

Biblical Foundation

In those days a decree went out from Emperor Augustus that all the world should be registered. This was the first registration and was taken while Quirinius was governor of Syria. All went to their own towns to be registered. Joseph also went from the town of Nazareth in Galilee to Judea, to the city of David called Bethlehem, because he was descended from the house and family of David. He went to be registered with Mary, to whom he was engaged and who was expecting a child. While they were there, the time came for her to deliver her child. And she gave birth to her firstborn son and wrapped him in bands of cloth, and laid him in a manger, because there was no place for them in the inn. (Luke 2:1-7)

Special Preparation

- Get hymnals with the carol "Silent Night."

- Try to get a recording of the Simon and Garfunkel song "7 O'Clock News / Silent Night" from the 1966 album *Parsley, Sage, Rosemary, and Thyme*. The song can also be purchased online or there are several YouTube clips.

- Get copies of current newspapers, or download and make copies of news stories for this week from the Internet. You will need scissors, glue, and some large sheets of paper.

- Andrew Peterson's song "Labor of Love" is available on the Internet—either lyrics or video. You will need the equipment to show it in video form.

- Prepare four posterboard "gift boxes." Use wide ribbon to tie a large bow and attach to the top, or cut a bow from colored pasteboard and attach to the top. Head each sheet with one of the following: The Gift of the Way; The Gift of Love; The Gift of Forgiveness and New Life; The Gift of the Resurrection. A more elaborate way of doing this activity is to wrap four large cartons as gifts and attach posterboard sheets to the sides. The finished "gifts" can then be stacked in a hallway or gathering area where they can be read.

- On a large sheet of paper, print the titles and Scriptures of all five sessions in this study: 1. Beginning with the End (Acts 1:8-14); 2. The Piercing of Mary's

Soul (Luke 2:33-35); 3. Amazed, Astounded, and Astonished (Luke 2:41-51); 4. Mary, Full of Grace (Luke 1:26-33); and 5. It Was Not a Silent Night (Luke 2:1-7). If possible, briefly review the sessions to recall the themes. Leave room between the titles for printing observations and reflections.

- Place a white candle in the center of the Advent wreath.

- A study cited in the book found that two-thirds of women who were asked reported experiencing depression during the holidays, and it is likely that a similar number of men do as well. Chances are good, therefore, that some people in your group are depressed. Be on the lookout for signs in participants, and make sure to point to the light and hope Christ brings to a suffering world.

- Remember that there are more activities than most groups will have time to complete. As leader, you'll want to go over the session in advance and select or adapt the activities you think will work best for your group in the time allotted.

Getting Started

Opening Activity

- Gather together and welcome participants and any newcomers. Invite them to peruse the newspapers or news stories you've brought and select headlines of current world, national, and local news. Have them glue the headlines to newsprint sheets to make a collage (or participants can print the headlines).

- The lyrics of "Silent Night" and other familiar carols have shaped the way we imagine the first Christmas, and yet our own Christmases seldom measure up.

- Explain that the group will now hear a recording that presents the sharp contrast between the Christmas ideal and reality. It is the final track on *Parsley, Sage, Rosemary, and Thyme*, a 1966 album by Simon and Garfunkel. The track consists of overdubbing two contrasting recordings: a simple arrangement of the Christmas carol "Silent Night" and a simulated "7 O'Clock News" bulletin of the actual events of August 3, 1966. Play the track or show the video.

- Invite the group to sing or recite "Silent Night," while at the same time participants read the current headlines they themselves chose.

Opening Prayer

Light the candles on the Advent wreath (or the white pillar candle if this session happens after the last week of Advent) with the words "Come, Lord Jesus." Allow for a time of silence. Then pray:

Come, Lord Jesus. In the midst of this messy, challenging world in which we live, come. In the midst of darkness, pain, and suffering, come. As you were born into a similar world, come. We await the life and love you bring. In your name we pray. Amen.

Learning Together

Video Study and Discussion

In Session 5, we come full circle with Mary and find ourselves at the manger, just after Jesus' birth. We consider the question "Was it really a silent night?" from the perspective of Mary and then, finally, for us.

Before viewing the video, ask participants to imagine having to walk miles and miles over dusty roads when nearly ready to give birth. How might Mary have felt under those circumstances? What conversations might Mary and Joseph have had along the way?

After viewing the video, ask participants to consider their ideal Christmas—the sights, sounds, and feelings. Discuss:

- Where does our image of the perfect Christmas come from? Has anyone in the group ever actually experienced it? What Christmas came the closest? What Christmas was the least perfect?

- What can we learn from Mary's experience at Christmas—not the imaginary Christmas of "Silent Night" but the real Christmas that Mary must have had?

- Looking beyond Christmas, what other times in our lives do we hope and expect to be perfect? How might we adjust those expectations, and how would it affect our experience of God in those situations?

Bible and Book Study and Discussion

Comparing and Contrasting Childbirth Practices

Ask the group to read over the information under the book heading "Not Silent in Bethlehem." Invite mothers or grandmothers in the group to answer the following about their experiences of childbirth:

- Who was present at your child's birth, and who came to help you after you went home?

- Where were your children born? Who delivered them?

- What kinds of services were available to you during and after the birth of your children?

Invite someone to summarize what was learned in the book about conditions for childbirth in the first century. What were some of the hazards involved? Have someone read from the book the description of a modern hospital birthing room. Discuss:

- Hamilton suggests we might think of the place Mary gave birth to Jesus as a first-century parking garage. What does he mean? Why does he suggest that it was anything but a silent night?

Hamilton mentions the Andrew Peterson song "Labor of Love." You now can play the YouTube clip or audio file.

Hear Scripture

Explain that for most of us, the reading and hearing of today's Scripture passage is a treasured part of our Christmas observance. But often its very familiarity means it is more difficult to encounter Scripture in new ways. Invite the group to keep in mind the discussion they just had about birthing practices and the hazards and dangers involved for a mother in the first century. Ask them also to keep in mind how Mary might have felt about giving birth away from her mother and others in the community. Then ask them to close their eyes and listen as you read Scripture aloud, seeking to hear it in fresh ways.

The Gifts of Christmas

Hamilton discusses what he calls the real gifts of Christmas, which he says are the reasons he follows Jesus. Form four smaller groups or pairs and give to each group one of the posterboard "gift boxes." Ask them to read the information about their gift and to print on the box a few comments about the gift. Then ask them to respond to the following:

- How have you experienced this gift or seen it lived out in the life of another?

- What practices might we begin or continue in order to embrace this gift after Christmas is over?

After allowing time for groups to discuss and create their gift boxes, have each group report. If possible, display the gift boxes where other congregants can read them and reflect on the gifts of Christmas.

Wrapping Up

Review with the group what they explored over the past five weeks about Mary and what was revealed by using her life and experiences as a lens through which to view Christmas. Call the group's attention to the large sheet on which you've written the session titles. Consider each session title and Scripture in turn, and invite the group to summarize each in a sentence or two.

Ask participants to discuss which of the suggested follow-up faith activities and spiritual practices they tried over the course of the study. Invite them to reflect on which ones they might want to continue after Christmas. For example, what other phrases might work as breath prayers? How might participants deepen their practice of hospitality with vulnerable people? How can prayer practices and regular Scripture reading help make the connection between cradle and cross more clear? How can participants add faith practices that help them follow Jesus' example of how to live?

Closing Activity

Light the Advent candles one last time. Also light the white pillar candle and remind the group that this candle is the Christ candle, symbolizing the coming of Jesus Christ, the light of the world. Invite a volunteer to read aloud the final two book paragraphs under the heading "A Silent Night After All."

Sing "Silent Night" together.

Closing Prayer

We thank you, O God, for the gift of Jesus Christ. By your Spirit, guide us as we seek to follow him, trust in his love, allow him to save us from ourselves, and put our hope in him. As we seek to more faithfully follow your way, make us your instruments to bring your light into the world. Amen.